The Truth Of The World

AF271673

pawan kumar saini

ISBN 978-93-5458-833-4
© pawan kumar saini 2021
Published in India 2021 by Pencil

A brand of
One Point Six Technologies Pvt. Ltd.
123, Building J2, Shram Seva Premises,
Wadala Truck Terminal, Wadala (E)
Mumbai 400037, Maharashtra, INDIA
E connect@thepencilapp.com
W www.thepencilapp.com

Author biography

I was born in a farmer's family in Rajasthan and we are five brothers, the eldest I am I did my 10th from Balbharti Senior Secondary School Kotputli in my hometown and Passed graduation from L.B.S.P.G. KotputliI was born in a farmer's family in Rajasthan and we are five brothers, the eldest I am I did my 10th from Balbharti Senior Secondary School Kotputli in my hometown and Passed graduation from L.B.S.P.G. Kotputli

CONTENTS

Author biography..3

flaws in you dear.......................................7

the way...9

Distance of fear......................................10

A Man Life 11

flaws in you 13

our beautiful world..................................15

passed way...17

Wrong Person...18

Great Person 19

walked the way.......................................20

never fall In love friend..21

The Life Of A Man 23

Debauchery..25

O My Heart If You Had Been Some Aware 26

Who Claim..29

Don't Try To Hew Us 30

Who has Seen In Whose Heart 31

Himself A mirror..32

Compulsion 33

What Kind Of Yearn Is..34

Tears 36

Burnt My desires 37

कभी हस्ते थे दोनो एक साथ में 38

क्या होता है इन्सान 39

जिल्लत क्या खूब की 40

अच्छा इन्सान 41

बेवफा 42

टूटकर चाहना..43

तुथ्कर चाहने की बात...44

Thank You 45

flaws in you dear

Who says you have flaws in you dear

Between dream and reality is flowing water of fear

The story is the thinking to go an end

Thinking of both only goes to an end

One is weak and the other is wise friend

On useless different things thinking of the weak spend

The weaker have only one trend

Sometime is to get beautiful girlfriend

Sometime to earn much and to buy land

To one thing all day thinking of the wise spend

Walks every day in dreams gets the destination

One who landed in reality from dreams?

In every heart fear of "I can't do "seems

Look this world is made in really by dreams

Taaj mahal, red Fort or four beams

Before making someone thought in dreams

Everything of this world is written on imagination

Digit, letter directions and formulation

Everything is going on writing on imagination

Truth is written by knowing formation

the way

Take step ahead at least,

The way will be build itself

Bring dreams in reality at least

Feet will also cross the destination

Distance of fear

Who knows the distance of fear

between dream and reality

He can achieve everything

A Man Life

Man only shows off in his life

The show off of looking better than others

The show off of being beautiful and handsome than others

The show off of being better than others

The show off of working harder than others

The show off of earning more money than others

The show off of writing better than others

The show off of playing better than others

This is a human life

Human have no money, have only things

Spends according to he earns

The human plays with things

Money is only a source it is life of a human

flaws in you

Who says you have flaws in you dear

Between dream and reality is flowing water of fear

The story is the thinking to go an end

Thinking of both only goes to an end

One is weak and the other is wise friend

On useless different things thinking of the weak spend

The weaker have only one trend

Sometime is to get beautiful girlfriend

Sometime to earn much and to buy land

To one thing all day thinking of the wise spend

Walks every day in dreams gets the destination

One who landed in reality from dreams?

In every heart fear of "I can't do "seems

Look this world is made in really by dreams

Taaj mahal, red Fort or four beams

Before making someone thought in dreams

Everything of this world is written on imagination

Digit, letter directions and formulation

Everything is going on writing on imagination

Truth is written by knowing formation

our beautiful world

What a beautiful world has made by education

How Man has decorated it with his devotion

Man is going ahead with rule and law

Spreading education everywhere over the raw

War was only one art ancients have to show

After many people were killed, a great man became so

This have turned a means of security now

Football hockey and javelin throw

Today there are many arts a man has to show

Many people are also getting great in inventions wow

Today human speaks truth so much

Blind faith, lies and custom of untouch

There were things in ancient such

Every heart has become beautiful now

And sweetness is on every mow

How Man has decorated it with his devotion

Everything of this world is written on imagination

Digit, letter directions and formulation

Everything is going on writing on imagination

Truth is written by knowing formation

What a beautiful world has made by education

passed way

passed through this way

in the madness of love

who knew bitch life

will cry so much one day

Wrong Person

Look at the reason behind any person's speaking

Man's real meaning looks

If it's right, he'll be right

if it's wrong he'll be wrong

Great Person

Those who think others are bad are very small in thinking

can be judged from their talks

The true always speaks sweetly,

is great in thinking can be judged by their words

Because he weighs every person by himself

That's why he speaks most of the things with the right thinking

walked the way

One day Our heart was also opened

We Just walked along the way too

The eyes did not deceive , sir

, matter was of stubborn heart

never fall In love friend

Never fall in love friend

Heart breaks at the end

It begins to change trend

As a few days spend

This heart is innocent friend

Thinks it a godsend

Never fall in love friend

Heart breaks at the end

I understood to this heart just

When it fell in love at the first

Love is only a spring passing gust

I have lost everything in this lust

Never fall in love friend

Heart breaks at the end

In first rain of love, bliss blow

What happens next you don't know

At last sand of love turns fallow

And dream begins to break slow

The Life Of A Man

Man only shows off in his life

The show off of looking better than others

The show off of being beautiful and handsome than others

The show off of being better than others

The show off of working harder than others

The show off of earning more money than others

The show off of writing better than others

The show off of playing better than others

This is a human life

Human have no money, have only things

Spends according to he earns

The human plays with things

Money is only a source it is life of a human

,

Debauchery

Whose love is complete, sir

We just have some fun with the debauchery

O My Heart If You Had Been Some Aware

O my heart if you had been some aware

I had also been a some aware

This heart went on saying I just walked along the way

Who know Suborn heart will take me here one day

Speaking two sweet words

Destroying dream's world

Like this way to drop through the eyes no one dare

O my heart if you had been some aware

I had also been a some aware

Sometime you walk with winds sometime in mist

Looking drown in love I said "listen to me at least"

I wanted to stop thee

How you listen to me

But mash of wanting love climbed on you bare

O my heart if you had been some aware

I had also been a some aware

The color of love had got climbed in every vein

Many raptures arose in heart, took me in bliss then

I will live with you end of the doom day

Like a shadow she used to say

When I came into dark night that shadow
disappear

O my heart if you had been some aware

I had also been a some aware

Who Claim

Deception, lies and unfaithfulness,

everything is in this world

Well someone would make a claim

to tell his this truth

Don't Try To Hew Us

o life weare ourselves a mirror

don't try to hew us

Who has Seen In Whose Heart

Who has seen in whose heart?

Without any reason

rumors are flying about being unfaithful

We just insisted on persuading once

Himself A mirror

a person is himself the mirror of others

One who looks himself,sees others

No person is bad, situations are like this

A person can make others blind, not himself

Man always has a sense of his own how much i am

Compulsion

Compulsion makes a person handicapped

hobby makes a person expert

What Kind Of Yearn Is

What kind of yearn is

What kind of mourn is

What kind turn is?

What kind of lorn is?

I am here vain

My feet have become own chain

These give only pain

Tell me someone how to abstain

Though ties of love have broken

Yet where these remain

How do these give pain

Through my eyes these rain

I am here wound

Far from there isn't ground

Where ocean is surround

Tears

Tears come out of human soul only twice

Once when he knows deception of truth

Twice when someone dies

Burnt My desires

What happened she burnt my desires in crowd

At least the Few hearts have got the light

कभी हस्ते थे दोनों एक साथ में

कभी हस्ते थे दोनों एक साथ में

हम ना बदलेंगे कहते थे बात ही बात में

बदलते देखा मैंने उसको भी दुःख की बरसात में

जैसे परछाई साथ छोड़ देती है अन्देरी रात में

क्या होता है इन्सान

एक दुसरे का आयना होता है इन्सान

खुद को देखकर आयने में सब को पहचान

खुद जैसा ही दूसरा होता है इन्सान

कोई बुरा नहीं है इस दुनिया में इन्सान

मैं उसके लिए ये करूँगा

मैं उसको ये ला के दूंगा

देख क्या सोचता है हर इन्सान

जिल्लत क्या खूब की

उस दिन हमने खुद की जिल्लत क्या खूब की

वो बोलते गए बाते पत्थर जैसे चूब की

फिर भी हमने रिश्ते को बनाने की कोशिश खूब की

हर कोशिश लग रही थी जैसे मानो धुब की

तब जाके समझ आया जब जाते देखा उनके चेहरे पर ख़ुशी शुभ की

क्या हद कर दी थी हमने भी उस दिन बेवकूफ की

अच्छा इन्सान

अगर तुम्हे तुमारा दिल बहुत खुबसूरत लगता है

तो तुम एक अछे इन्सान हो

बेवफा

दिल चिर कर किसने किसका देखा है साहब

बेवजह अफवाह उड़ रही है बेवफा होने की

हमने तो जिद की थी एक बार मनाने की

टूटकर चाहना

वो इस दिल को टूटकर चाहने के तज़ुर्बे तो बहुत सिखा गए

कोई जला ना सके जालिम को इसलिए नाम खुद का लिखा गए

तुथ्कर चाहने की बात

फिर याद आई तुम्हारी दिल कराहने लगा

छलक आये आंसू फिर मेरे

सोचा बसा लेगे किसी और को दिल में

पर द्दिल में वो टूटकर चाहने की बात नहीं आई

Thank You

enjoy your life according to you